Looking at Light

Contents

Different kinds of light

There are lots of different kinds of light.

Do you know what makes light?

Light from electricity

Lamps and lights in our houses give
electric light.

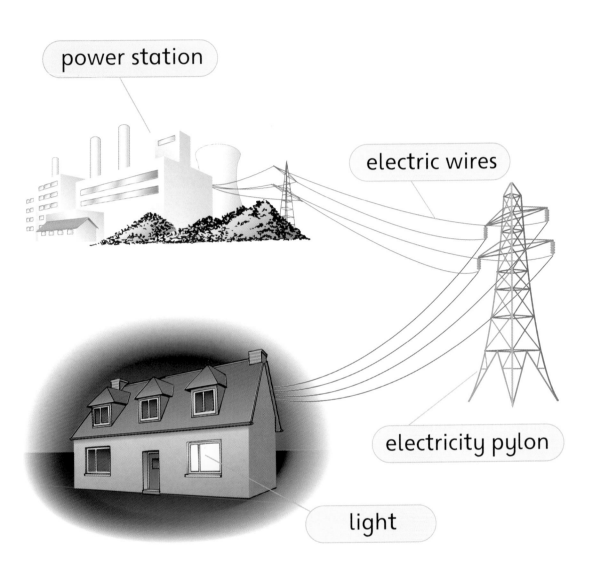

power station

electric wires

electricity pylon

light

They use electricity to give light.

Electricity is a type of energy.

Light from batteries

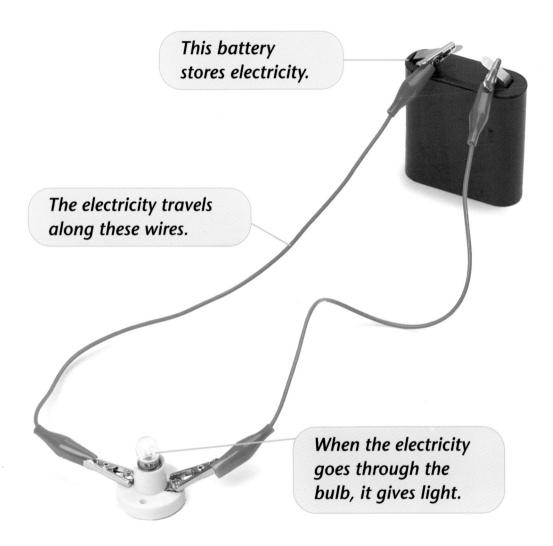

This battery stores electricity.

The electricity travels along these wires.

When the electricity goes through the bulb, it gives light.

Batteries store electricity.

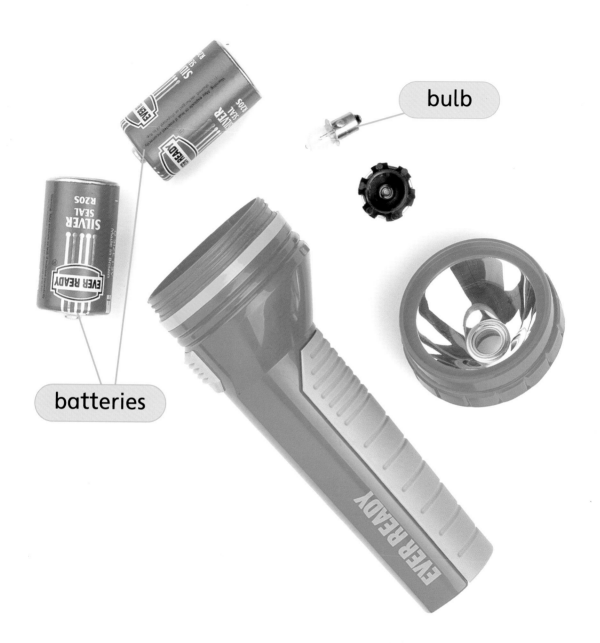

bulb

batteries

A torch uses batteries and a bulb to make light.

Light from fire

Matches make firelight.

Candles use fire to make light.
Sometimes we use firelight when there
is no electric light.

Light from the Sun

Light comes from the Sun.

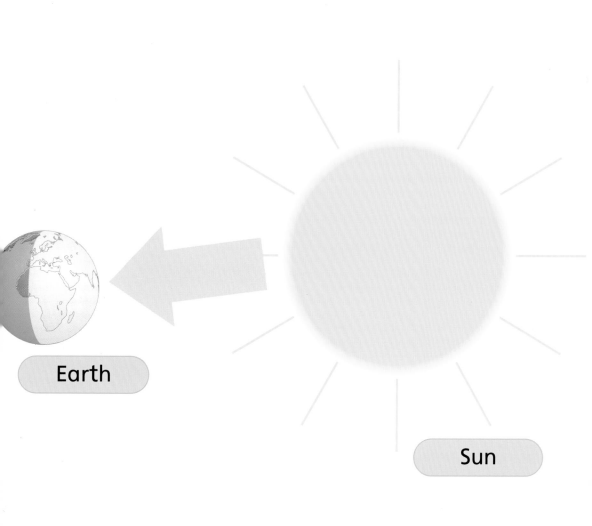

Earth

Sun

The Sun is a ball of fire. It shines down on the Earth. On a sunny day it can be very hot.

Light from the Moon

Light comes from the Moon.

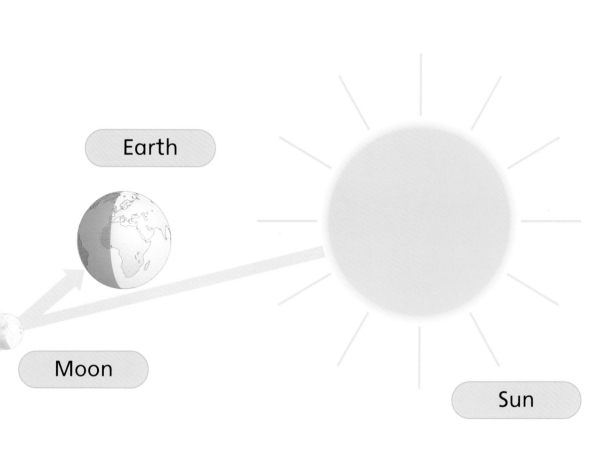

Earth

Moon

Sun

The Moon is like a big mirror. Light from the Sun bounces off the Moon back to Earth. It makes the Moon shine at night.

Light chart

Light from electricity	Light from batteries

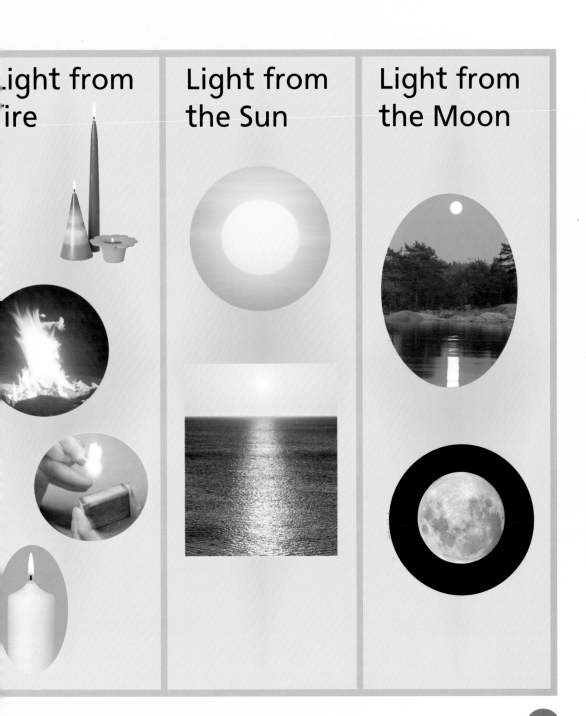

Light from fire

Light from the Sun

Light from the Moon

a
b
c
d
e
f
g
h
i
j
k
l
m
n
o
p
q
r
s
t
u
v
w
x
y
z

Index